Mother & Child

ༀ་མ་ཎི་པ་དྨེ་ཧཱུྃ

for Mingma

Mother & Child

VISIONS OF PARENTING
FROM INDIGENOUS CULTURES

JAN REYNOLDS

INNER TRADITIONS INTERNATIONAL
ROCHESTER, VERMONT

INNER TRADITIONS INTERNATIONAL

ONE PARK STREET
ROCHESTER, VERMONT 05767
Web Site: http://www.gotoit.com

LIBRARY OF CONGRESS CATALOGING-IN-PUBLICATION DATA

Reynolds, Jan, 1956–

Mother & child : visions of parenting from indigenous cultures / Jan Reynolds.

p. cm.

ISBN 0-89281-637-6

1. Mother and child—Cross-cultural studies. 2. Parenting—Cross-cultural studies.

I. Title.

HQ759.R49 1997   96-32597

306.874'3—dc20   CIP

Printed in Hong Kong

10 9 8 7 6 5 4 3 2 1

Book design by Bonnie Atwater
Art direction by Tim Jones

This book was typeset in Weiss with Phaistos and Lucida Sans as display typefaces

Distributed to the book trade in Canada by Publishers Group West (PGW), Toronto, Ontario
Distributed to the book trade in the United Kingdom by Deep Books, London
Distributed to the book trade in Australia by Millennium Books, Newtown, N.S.W.
Distributed to the book trade in New Zealand by Tandem Press, Auckland
Distributed to the book trade in South Africa by Alternative Books, Randburg

(OPPOSITE)   *Life in the Yurts, in the high summer pastures for the Kirkiz.*

(NEXT PAGE)   *Taking a rest after spinning the prayer wheel at the monastery.*

contents

introduction

MOTHERS ARE THE ESSENCE of tomorrow. A mother's interaction with her child shapes the way her child will treat others in the future. She instills self-esteem in her child, offering an enduring love that enables her child to love himself. A mother teaches the earliest and deepest lessons, those of lasting emotional value.

How can she do this? Mothering is a progression, not a singular event. It is like becoming an artist or a musician: we improve with experience and by following natural instincts. Throughout pregnancy and childbirth a woman is driven to dig deep into herself for an inner strength she had not known existed. After birth, the smell of her baby opens a mother's soul to a new intimacy. She has crossed the threshold into motherhood.

(*OPPOSITE*)

Summer shade for

Asu in the Sahara.

From now on her child is constantly in her thoughts. Every decision she must make affects the well-being of her child. She learns the true meaning of sacrifice and giving.

I have had the privilege of living with indigenous mothers around the world and of seeing first hand their age-old ways of loving and teaching their children. I learned from these mothers that the natural world has eternity in it, and a mother's instincts during pregnancy, birth, and child rearing links her to this eternal chain of life.

While living with mothers from the Himalaya, the Sahara, Finmark, the Aboriginal Outback, the Amazon territory, above the Arctic Circle, and Mongolia, I saw that their guiding hands and basic lives gave so much to their children. They taught their children through example to grow confident, caring, and con-

mother & child

nected with their natural environment. The indigenous women that I met as I traveled taught me and influenced my life, even before I myself became a mother.

In my seventh month of pregnancy I traveled to Mani Rumdu, the largest festival in the Himalaya Mountain range surrounding the world's highest peak, Chomoluma, Mother Goddess of Earth. Jay, my future husband, and I were going to stay with my Sherpa friends Anu and Mingma, whose extended families have traversed the Himalaya from Nepal to Tibet as traders for as long as anyone can recall.

Neither Mingma nor I had sent word to the other that we were with child. We wanted to surprise each other. As I rounded a bend in the trail that

(*OPPOSITE*) *Mingma and her mother.*

(*THIS PAGE*) *I circumambulate clockwise around a Tibetan temple. Each morning pilgrims spin prayer wheels as they walk to create good fortune.*

led to her home, I spotted Mingma and she spotted me. We pointed at each other and began to laugh loudly. I had visited Mingma and her children many times before, but this was new. I had never seen her in this phase of her life, and this was my first pregnancy. Jay trekked in soon after me.

We had not yet married, but in Sherpa culture our timing was perfect—the Sherpas marry in three stages. First the husband-to-be moves in with his woman and her family. Provided all goes well, they then move into a house of their own. Finally, they have a big celebration and ceremony directed by the Lama from one of the nearby monasteries. Most often a child is either already born or on the way by the time of the celebration, so the couple knows that they can conceive.

In no time Mingma convinced us to let her put on our wedding. She felt we were ready for the last stage because Jay and I had already moved into our own home before we left for this trip to the Himalaya, and I was carrying our child. Mingma wanted to organize this celebration for us.

She dressed me in the robes of silk and brocade that she and her mother had worn at their weddings. Jay wore Mingma's brother-in-law's gorgeous silks. We were married with my extended family in the Himalaya in attendance—over fifty of Mingma's relatives joined the celebration. The Lama from the Tenboche monastery read from an ancient book of Tibetan text, and we were married as auspicious hail pelted the roof.

mother & child

Everyone clapped at this rare sign of good fortune!

It felt right to be married in the heart of the Himalaya, and to be with Mingma for the next week when she gave birth, in her own home, to her baby girl Rosine. In this book you will meet Mingma and other great women whom I have spent time with. The close connection these women have with the natural world gives them the confidence to connect with their own offspring and to trust in their natural instincts while handling them. They speak with words that carry wisdom from generation to generation, with actions worthy of our attention.

ceremony & celebration

Before motherhood, most commonly there is a form of marriage. Weddings can be as long and involved as the three-stage wedding that can span a year or two in the Himalaya, or as simple as hanging hammocks together in the thatched hut shapono housing for extended families in the Amazon territory. All events are respected for what they signify: the union of the man and the woman, becoming husband and wife as we know it.

Before motherhood there is, of course, pregnancy. The woman, and only the woman, will be with child. This indisputable ability belongs solely to her. Before she gives birth to her child and passes through the transition to motherhood, she lives

with pregnancy for nine months. During this time she becomes a sacred vessel, becomes the natural link in the continuation of her people, becomes part of the chain of human life. For indigenous people, ceremony and celebration often surround marriage and pregnancy. These rites of passage are acknowledged and revered for recognizing these transitions in a woman's life. They lend her confidence in her new role as wife and mother.

mother & child

A TUAREG MARRIAGE IN THE SAHARA AND A
YANOMAMA's PREGNANCY IN THE AMAZON

THE MARRIAGE CELEBRATION of the Tuareg, deep in the heart of the Sahara, has always fascinated me because in that society it is the women who choose the men. It is a matrilineal society—as they say, "It is the belly that holds the child." Therefore it is the woman who passes on the family wealth and the name. Another twist is that the men wear veils, not the women. When I repeatedly asked the men why this is, I would receive the same answer, "Why, because we are Tuareg."

Famous for their courtship, the Tuareg perform the Illugan, or camel dance. The veiled men wear turbans of white and deep indigo fabric, which winds down around their faces. They ride around the women, who are clustered together clapping and singing. During the Illugan a woman selects a suitor by the way he rides a camel, so the story goes, because all that the women can see of the men are charcoal-darkened eyes under veils, and flowing robes. As the men prance

their camels around the singing women, they are chosen, one by one. When a woman has found her proper suitor, the wedding takes a couple of days and nights to perform.

I had made my way across Algeria into the very center of the Sahara, where the Tuareg still dwell. Through a friend with whom I could speak French, I had been invited to a genuine Tuareg wedding— something very few outsiders have ever participated in.

I arrived for the evening camel dancing and awoke in the middle of the night to the sound of a heavy drumbeat and an intricate kind of choral singing. The night was heavy with stars, and without external lights or moisture to diffuse the darkness, falling stars streaked across the sky like many tiny rockets.

The next day the women cooked a great feast, singing as they worked. The men had a tea ceremony during which their holy man spoke with the fathers of those to be married. He asked for any objections from the crowd. After the great feast, there was camel dancing at sunset. That night I awoke to what sounded like a swarm of bees and an exotic drumbeat in the background. The men were circling three camel-leather tents, one housing the groom, who was all dressed in white.

Off in the distance, the women approached from their campfires, singing in response to the men. The women offered some sandals to the men upon meeting, and the men playfully declined to let them pass. Something else was offered that I could not see, perhaps a wooden spoon or some other simple everyday item. The men let the women pass

mother & child

by and circled the three tents, singing, as the bride, dressed in white, entered the tent where the groom was waiting. This was only a visit, but the woman knew that soon she would have this man's children, although they would have her name, and she would pass the family riches on to her daughters.

It wasn't until the next night, after the men had prepared the evening feast and the camel dancing and racing had finished that the bride and groom left together to sleep in their own tent. This would become their home, as it is for all nomadic societies. Everyone struck camp the following morning to continue their separate lives, but the Tuareg lineage would continue through this newly married woman, and soon with a new life.

mother & child

THERE IS MORE CEREMONY and celebration surrounding pregnancy than the actual marriage for the Yanomama in the Amazon territory. Marriage simply occurs when the couple hang their hammocks side by side next to their own fire. But women with child dance and sing their heris, which are songs of thanks and gratitude. They dance in front of all the others living in their shapono—about fifty people—accentuating the changes taking place in their bodies.

The Yanomama live as far into the Amazon territory as do the Tuareg into the Sahara, and this has allowed them to retain their cultural ways until recently. But now, because of the discovery of gold on their land, it has been infiltrated by fortune seekers, and the Yanomama's future is more uncertain. For me, watching and listening to the heris lifted my spirit. And to see the pregnant women dancing with joy gave me hope for the Yanomama's survival.

The women who are with child go down by a river fed by a cold spring to have themselves decorated. A long, green leaf that becomes

(THIS PAGE) Deep in the Amazon Basin the triple-canopy jungle is so thick that one can travel only on the water.

(OPPOSITE) Pregnant woman is decorated for dancing heris.

mother & child

sticky when wet is rubbed over their hair so their heads can be covered with tiny down feathers. Deep red onoto seeds are mixed with ashes from the fire to make stylized black body paintings, and long, stiff grasses are inserted into pierced holes along the mouth and through the septum of the nose. Reeds with brightly colored feathers are inserted in the ears, and grasses are tied around the arms. I thought the women looked exquisite, especially when I could let go of my society's concepts of beauty.

The women dance by the shapono, moving forward and back, holding their breasts and singing loudly. Their dances flaunt their changing shape. Many other women and children follow along behind them as they circle the shapono, repeating their steps and song after them. The little girls charmed me with their imitations of the older women. They had an air of strength and maturity. This dancing seemed to me to be a celebration of the lineage of the tribe passing down through the women. It reminded me of the Tuareg women circling the bride's tent, knowing that they carry the lineage of their tribe as well, and of the unspoken chain of life passed on by all women around the world.

birth

Throughout time mothers have instinctively given birth at home and nursed their babies. The indigenous mothers who befriended me taught me the value of this intimate, initial connection to their babies, inspiring me to do the same.

When a child first enters the world it experiences perhaps the greatest shock of its entire life. All senses are newly engaged: there is light, unmuffled noise, a change in temperature, and dry, maybe drafty, air. There is empty space surrounding the flailing body, and the loud sound of the baby's own cry wails in its ears.

And there is taste. Mother's nipple and milk may well be the only consolation for a newborn making the headlong plunge into this adventure called life. This gave me reason enough to nurse my baby even before his dad cut the umbilical chord at our home birth.

With home birth the newborn is held and nursed by the mother all through the first night; there is no separation. In this

way, the Mother's heartbeat continues to give comfort. It is the only thing that remains consistent and stable for the baby in his changing world, for even the mother's voice sounds different now.

My indigenous friends, mothers themselves in remote environments, showed me that they were their child's sensual connection to the new world that surrounded their baby. A baby does not distinguish itself as an entity separate from its mother for several months, and intuitively my friends handled their babies as if they were still part of their own person. For them, the birth of a child did not signify a beginning or an ending. It was merely a major event in the continuation of the child's life, so a birth at home, or feeding at the mother's breast, seemed to be the most natural continuation of a baby's worldly existence.

This continued, intimate bond between mother and child

mother & child

after birth seemed natural and complete to me. In the Amazon, the Himalaya, the Sahara, and other far corners of the world I saw newborns either nursed, held, or carried in some fashion by their mothers from the moment of birth. Mother and child were still connected. The baby was given every human signal that would nurture a sense of security during its most vulnerable stage of life.

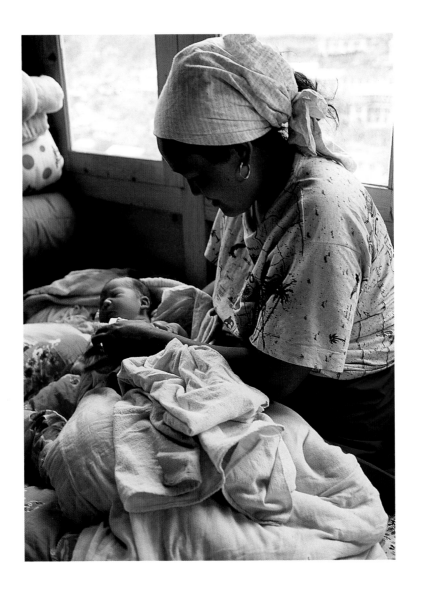

HOME BIRTH AND NURSING WITH THE SHERPAS AND
KIRKIZ IN THE HIMALAYA MOUNTAIN CHAIN

MY HIMALAYAN FRIENDS Anu and Mingma had a home that was primitive by modern standards but cozy and clean. There was one open fire in the kitchen area, where fresh stream water was brought in for cooking. The house itself was made from stone chipped and shaped to fit without the use of mortar.

Just one week after Mingma had orchestrated our Zendi, the wedding, she gave birth to a beautiful, fat, baby girl. I never knew that Mingma was in labor. She kept it from everyone but Anu, her husband. One day I detected something different about Mingma's demeanor but couldn't define it. In the evening she walked around outside, almost pacing, while talking with Anu. I thought they were having an intense, personal conversation and stayed clear.

It wasn't until the middle of that night that I figured out what was going on. The low soft moans escaping from the room above ours left me with no doubt that labor had progressed and the birth of the baby was imminent.

Very soon afterward, we heard a soft laugh coming from Mingma. Rosine had been born. I could hear Anu speaking, and also Mingma's mother. Apparently people had called out from window to window in the night that it was time for Namdu, Mingma's mother, to come. It was a beautiful birth, with the mother aiding and comforting her daughter as she gave birth to her own new baby girl. Although the baby had entered the world and become physically separated from her mother, she still had all of the warmth and security her mother could provide. Rosine was laid at Mingma's breast, able to rest, nurse, and hear her mother's voice and heartbeat. Birth therefore became more of a change in environment than a separation between people.

I anxiously waited until dawn before going down to the fireside to congratulate Anu, hoping all the while to see the baby but not daring to ask. Anu had been busy stoking the fire through the night, boiling water and providing Namdu with whatever she needed to facilitate the birth. He immediately ushered Jay and me to where mother and baby lay contentedly wrapped in blankets on the floor of a tiny room with no furniture. The accommodations were simple, but Mingma and Rosine were thriving. Mother and child were spotless and in good health, and the room was very tidy. The miracle of birth had blossomed in the Himalaya.

mother & child

IN THE PAMIR MOUNTAINS, a northern spur of the Himalayan chain, I lived with another group of mountain people very similar to the Sherpas, called the Kirkiz. I befriended a woman named Tursunai when I climbed Mustagata, one of the highest peaks in this range, almost 25,000 feet high.

When I first met Tursunai, she was inside her yurt, happily nursing her toddler. Her ruddy skin glowed from the high-altitude sun, and she smiled so easily that I felt instantly at home with her. She was not a bit abashed or apologetic

(OPPOSITE) *Mingma and newborn.*

(THIS PAGE) *Tursunai, escaping the heat of the day, nurses her child in the cool quiet of her yurt.*

BIRTH

about baring her breast in front of a stranger to feed her child—
nursing for her was as common as getting a drink of water. We
studied each other laughingly, curiously fingering each other's
belongings and clothing. We eventually traded earrings, perhaps
wishing to give something of ourselves to each other.

She beckoned for me to come with her and her children as she
went out of the yurt. Throughout the day I sensed Tursunai's
connection with the sheep and goats she tended. And beyond this
I felt her strong connection to her family. Tursunai's life was a
tightly connected web of interdependence. I could see that this
sense of interdependence, such a strong force in Tursunai's life, was
transferred to her children as they played alongside her while she
went about her daily chores.

When Tursunai drove the goats together and began milking
them, I saw a clear example of the balance of her connection to the
land and the animals. She herded the goats to the greener pastures
for their sustenance, while the goats provided her family with milk,
meat, and hair for the felt that covered their yurts.

When we returned to the yurt, I watched as Tursunai held her
toddler to her breast again. To me, the intimate bond that she
continued with her child exemplified the interdependence and the
spirit of the natural web that connected her to the land and the
animals.

Although Tursunai's child could walk, I could see that he wasn't
quite secure in his world. Most probably his nutritional needs

could be met with the local diet, yet he continued to feed at the breast. The other women living in this cluster of yurts were nursing their toddlers as well. I felt that Tursunai and the other women were offering unconditional warmth as they nursed their children, giving them the security and stability they needed in their broadening world.

Many of the other women and their youngest ones came into the yurt to sit with us. They told me a great legend of the gods and goddesses in flowing white robes who tend the luscious fruit gardens on the summit of Mustagata, the sacred peak that I had just climbed. This legend taught me much about these women's values.

Speaking symbolically, the gardens of the story were their own personal gardens, the lush fields and the flowers that flourished because of the clean, clear water source flowing down from the sacred mountain. Perhaps the gods and goddesses in flowing white robes were the blessed snows that fall year-round at the top of the mountain, feeding the water source, which indeed nourishes the gardens. I felt that Tursunai and the other women were trying to tell me that it isn't so important to climb the mountain as it is to understand the mountain's natural wealth, and to treat it with the respect it deserves as a life-giving force.

Many of the women sat cross-legged, nursing their children in their laps as the story was told. I saw them as a life-giving source as well, tending their children so that they could grow strong and sure. By nursing their young ones while they still wobbled on their newfound legs, these mothers gave their children a continuing link of security as they moved from their most vulnerable stage of life out into the ever-changing world.

3

still attached

A busy mother working close to the land and the animals does not want to leave her baby alone, away from her and her work. Indigenous mothers whom I lived with had a way of strapping their infants to themselves as they went about their daily chores. As I watched the mothers move about, intent upon their work, their precious load didn't appear to be a hindrance or a burden.

And for the baby, life is warm, welcoming, safe, and highly stimulating. From its first hours onward, the baby participates in its cultural lifestyle, although vicariously. The jostle and bustle of activity, and the sounds and smells that go along with it, are experienced firsthand by the infant, most likely becoming cataloged as the framework for the child's decision-making in the future.

Although carrying the baby is a pragmatic solution to caring for an infant while working, the mother's personal and physical attachment to the infant has emotional and developmental value. Whether the baby swings in a sling or is strapped to the back, it is able to watch the mother's hands as they labor, watch the fire as it burns, and see others interacting with the mother. One of these babies might find our common mobile in a crib a little boring after riding along and exploring everything with its mother.

Sleep comes and goes while the baby is carried throughout the day. The mother doesn't bother to put the infant down when it nods off. This is another demonstration of these mothers' continuing attachment to their children, even after they are outside

mother & child

the womb. After all, it takes nine months of carrying before a baby is born, and perhaps a continuation of this closeness eases the infant into childhood.

At night, when it is time for the whole family to sleep, the baby is laid down to rest as well. The indigenous families that I lived with usually all slept together. Of course the baby is not in a sling or strapped to the back, but still it remains attached while curled up with its mother and the rest of the family.

THE CARRYING OF INFANTS FOR ALL TASKS
WITH THE INUIT OF THE ARCTIC

THE WIND BLEW, unchecked, across Big Lake, or Quamanituaq as the Inuit call it. Situated north and west of Canada's Hudson Bay, this area is known for being consistently the coldest spot on earth. But for my friend Akak, ice fishing out on the vast frozen surface was nothing out of the ordinary. She offered to take me ice fishing with her one cold, clear day. I agreed, but wondered what she would do with her infant while we fished in this harsh environment.

As we readied ourselves to brave the elements I watched Akak searching through caribou skin anoraks. An anorak is a hooded, pullover coat. We borrowed the name for this type of garment from the Inuit themselves, during the times of the early exploration in these areas. Akak pulled out a fur-lined, thigh-length anorak that she had made for herself. She had also made skin clothing for all of her family. Meanwhile, I dressed myself in the latest outdoor gear—polypropylene, fleece, down, and Gore-Tex—while Akak watched me quite skeptically.

We gathered fish line and all the other necessities for catching dinner. Then, as we were going out the door Akak grabbed her baby, Anautalik, who was barely old enough to sit up on her own, and slid the baby down the back of her anorak. I watched in amazement. I had climbed in the winter season in the Himalaya, but this blustery, moist cold here was more penetrating and severe. It stung. I didn't know the infant was going fishing too and was surprised, but I thought about it and realized that Inuit infants had participated in all events with their mothers in years past out of necessity. So of course they could do so today just as well.

Then I noticed that this anorak looked different, and queried Akak as we stepped out. This garment was called an amautik. There was extra room around her upper body, and the hood was extra large. All Inuit women had these garments for traveling with their infants in the frigid temperatures and howling winds. In days past they were made only out of caribou skin. The leather blocked the wind, and the fur of the animal gave efficient insulating warmth. Often the infant would be naked, lying next to the mother's skin inside the amautik. But Akak had designed a fabric amautik with a fur lining, and there was additional fur around Anautalik's face.

Akak told me that she wants to have her baby snuggled close to her, tucked under her hood, because she knows her baby is secure and cared for, rather than be without her while she works. Often Anautalik sleeps because of her

mother & child

mother's warmth inside the amautik generated by activity. With the help of the amautik, mother and child were able to stay united even in inhospitable conditions.

We jigged for fish under the ice through a hole that Akak had pounded open with a long sharp pole. We were successful, and I was frozen! Anautalik slept, then poked her head out of the hood for a brief time, looking like a fur-trimmed cherub. The softer wolf fur as a muff around her features caught her own body warmth and held it there, just in the vicinity of her face, so that she could watch what was going on in relative comfort.

The next day we were heading out to build an igloo, which is still used for hunting trips and travel in this area of the north. Akak insisted that I wear some of the skin clothing and boots that she had made, and I heartily concurred. Again Anautalik slid happily inside her mother's amautik, ready for anything that her mother wished to do. It appeared that being with her mother was all that mattered to Anautalik at this stage of her life. She was at ease, sleeping quietly or watching wide-eyed at all that happened around her. She never appeared threatened by events because she experienced them all vicariously through her mother from her secure perch.

I watched Akak and her husband search for the right spot to begin building. The snow had to be wind-packed to a perfect consistency for cutting blocks. To see Akak move, you would never have known she was carrying a baby in her amautik. She worked uninhibited, cutting and lifting the large chunks of snow. The inside of the entryway to the igloo was protected from the wind, and Anautalik popped her head out of the amautik to observe her mother packing snow between the blocks of the igloo. I laughed to think that education begins

mother & child

early here: before one can walk, one learns to build with blocks—really big blocks!

I began to understand how a child is born and cared for in this environment, which at first glance seems so impossible. The igloo walls of snow form a thick insulation, and oil lamps actually create enough heat for some warmth. Fires are built from twigs dug up from under the snow, although most meat and fish is eaten raw and frozen. The family sleeps together, often wrapped in musk ox skin, which is the warmest of all because the hairs are hollow, allowing for better insulation.

(ABOVE)

Inuit house cleaning.

(OPPOSITE) *Skin clothing makes living in this harsh environment possible.*

When I considered that a child is carried by the mother in her amautik until it is old enough to walk and be dressed in skins itself, the idea of infancy in this frozen world became plausible. Inside the igloo the child can crawl about, exploring different levels, furs, bone utensils, and more. Outside the child observes Inuit life in all its facets before it participates, growing safe and secure while riding on its mother's back.

After only about one hour the igloo was completed. Akak told me

mother & child

40

that this is how the Inuit clean house—they merely build a new igloo and leave the other one behind. For those people, who live in complete harmony with nature and natural processes, this custom works. When everything utilized by the culture comes from the land, it can simply return to the land and no harm is done.

STILL ATTACHED

41

In this habitat, referred to as the Barren Lands, the Inuit live alongside the other animals: arctic hare and tern, wolves, musk ox, and occasionally the frightful polar bear. Life for all beings in this frozen land is an obvious web of interdependence.

Akak's mother came to join the rest of the family in the igloo, bringing twigs

mother & child

for a fire so she could prepare tea to accompany the frozen fish we had brought along from our catch the day before. How warm it became with so many bodies inside! The igloo was a haven in an area where, when the wind blows on cold days, any exposed flesh will freeze within seconds.

Grandmother wore an amautik made entirely of skin, and Akak told me that she had been carried by her mother in an amautik just like this when she was an infant. I could see how Grandmother had passed an instinctual sense of mothering to her daughter. Now Akak passes this on to her own children as she holds Anautalik dear, carrying her along throughout the day and giving of herself to give her child a secure sense of her place in the world.

4

working side by side

Time has another definition in an indigenous society. Here work is an activity giving rhythm to life, not something that marks time in the passage of the day. Therefore it is very natural for a mother to take her toddler along with her during her daily chores. There is no enforced separation between generations—children are not shuttled off somewhere out of the way so that the adults can accomplish tasks without being interrupted. Mother and child work side by side, with the child assuming only as much of the task as he or she shows interest in.

A child's attention span correlates to the age of the child and doesn't seem to affect the mother's focus on the task at hand.

She guides the youngest if they express an interest, and directs those old enough to understand what needs to be accomplished. Here, children become familiar with the pattern and rhythm of their own culture or lifestyle very early, so it is natural for them to understand and accept work as an important part of a good life.

It seemed to me that a child performed more easily when taken along with the mother and given a chance. By including the child, the mother shows the child that he is not only wanted but needed, which in turn adds to the child's sense of belonging and sense of self-worth. Whether tending animals, planting crops, washing clothes, or trading goods, the indigenous children whom I lived with performed tasks alongside their mothers as a natural extension of their lives. The children learned and accepted their cultural ways and values through direct, tangible examples and participation. The loving guidance and response of the mother shaped her child's earliest perception of the world and his or her place within it.

mother & child

ON A DREAM JOURNEY WITH THE
ABORIGINES OF AUSTRALIA

AMPRENULA, a young girl who is part of the Tiwi Aboriginal group living on the islands just off the north coast of Australia, goes on Dream journeys with her mother and the rest of her extended family. The Dream journey travels on known, sacred routes, constantly in search of food. Amprenula has done this since she was born and able to toddle along on her own, and I had the good fortune to travel with her family one spring.

Amprenula showed me her spear. Made from the wood of a mangrove tree, it had been heated over the fire to give it additional strength to prevent splitting. A sharp spearhead had been shaped on one end, painted with natural pigments dug from the earth, and then baked in the fire to set the colors. This hunting tool can take down a wallaby thirty yards distant. Amprenula also carried palm baskets, which she slung over her shoulder on a throwing stick. These too were painted with traditional colors: the yellows, browns, and deep reds of Aboriginal Dreamtime art.

Amprenula told me about dugout canoes and the string bark huts her people had used until the missionaries arrived with prefabricated housing. The missionaries discouraged the Tiwi's own language and traditional customs, but because Amprenula's grandmother had continued to take her daughter out onto the land on Dream journeys, Amprenula was able to learn the old ways of her people from her own mother.

Amprenula had known how to tend a fire for as long as she could remember. Her mother had taught her because it is an essential skill for living out in the bush. I could see that Amprenula knew she belonged here as she worked with her mother to organize their bedding around the fire on the first night.

Amprenula's dark skin blended in with the night, but her eyes, opened wide and alert, seemed to glow white. The waiwai bird called out. All of this was familiar to Amprenula, since her mother had always taken her on the land to forage for food while traveling the songlines, the sacred traveling routes. She poked the glowing coals with a stick and fanned them so they would break into flame, then added more wood.

In the morning we were off early in search of breakfast, lunch, and dinner. The men had come back to the fires at dawn with a wallaby to share. But while they were skinning the animal, we women went looking for more. Amprenula took me under her wing, like many of the indigenous children I had met around the world, because she knew that I was ignorant about her world and this was her chance to be in charge.

She motioned for me to walk with her as we all foraged through the thinned forest. Her family had set a ground fire across this area early in the season to clear it for walking, and perhaps more importantly to allow for the growth of the fresh green shoots that drew wildlife to this area to feed. More wildlife means better hunting. Although Amprenula could speak English, she was more

(THIS PAGE) *mother and daughter*
pulling the sweet, juicy worms

(OPPOSITE) *Amprenula resting against an*
anthill while searching for food.

at home with her Tiwi language, so we spoke together very little while I simply shadowed her, imitating what she did when she motioned for me to do so.

Amprenula held out a broken piece of mirror to me as she got up off the ground. I wasn't sure what this was supposed to do until she put her hand over mine, moving the mirror back and forth so it reflected sunlight down the hollow log she had been kneeling beside. Then I saw it. There was a knot of scaly skin in the middle of the log—it was a snake. The huge serpent wouldn't budge when prodded with long sticks, so Amprenula called to her mother and grandmother to cut into the log to retrieve her snake. This would indeed make a good meal. Amprenula's mother smiled and assured her that she knew Amprenula could find some food for everyone.

mother & child

I realized that Amprenula was repeating her own previous experience by interacting with me just as she had with her own mother, although she had taken on the role of mother in our case. Through my friendship with Amprenula I was able to get a sense of her own learning process. In the past, by following her mother and mimicking her as her mother patiently waited, Amprenula had always been allowed to be a thread in the weave of their daily life. Now I was being allowed to do the same.

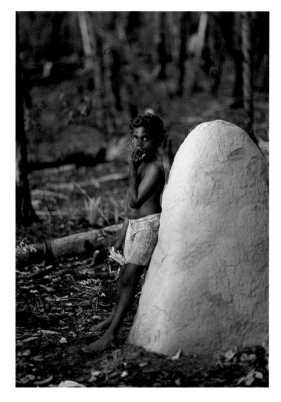

It was evident as we traveled how Amprenula's relationship to her mother and her environment had matured beyond simple observation. Now Amprenula queried her mother insistently all day. Down in the mangrove swamp they sat together, chipping off thick strips of bark from the dark, twisted mangrove trees. Amprenula watched as her mother pried open a piece, letting the sticky, clear juice that surrounded a worm run down over her hand.

Amprenula's mother had never made her feel like something other, different, or less important because she was a child while out on the

Dream journey. In fact, her mother had expected and assumed that Amprenula would be capable of the walk as well as active pursuit of game. However, Amprenula was always patiently waited for, or instructed when need be, so Amprenula's expectations of her mother were also met. What impressed me was that Amprenula was not fawned over, or wildly praised when she was helpful and alert, acting as her mother expected of her. Perhaps overt praise would have signaled to Amprenula that what she was doing was out of the ordinary, or exceptional, instead of simply expected, normal behavior.

I watched mother and child sucking worms together in the late afternoon heat of the mangrove swamp, sitting comfortably where crocodiles and snakes roam. Perhaps not many people would have seen it as a romantic scene, but to my eyes it was a bonding experience for Amprenula and her mother. Amprenula learned from her mother how to travel safely in this territory and how to find food here. Because of her mother, Amprenula had a sense of belonging in this land and of having a secure place in the world, as insecure as this world might seem to outsiders.

We moved on to look for sugarbag, or honeycomb, high in the trees while on our way back to our campsite, where roast snake and wallaby were waiting for us. Hunting during this long day was not work for Amprenula; this was merely her daily life when she traveled on songlines in the bush. Her personal part in this natural world was shaped by her mother's attention and response.

5

independence

I had seen the birth of a child in the Himalaya, infants nursed in the Sahara, babies carried inside Inuit amautiks far above the Arctic Circle, and toddlers and young children performing tasks as they played alongside their mothers in the Amazon territory. My first thought was that this close bond between mother and child would bring about the child's continued, strong dependence on the mother. But I observed the opposite. The children became confidently independent—a beautiful expression of personal freedom.

I noticed that as the toddlers grew they began to stray farther and farther from the mother. She would not run after them;

she even coolly expected them to follow her when she moved from chore to chore. She would always patiently wait, but would not necessarily coddle or cajole the child to follow along. Their bond was strangely unspoken; I often noticed mother and child staying in contact, casually keeping an eye on each other while minding their own tasks. This quiet stage was the link from dependence to independence.

After reflection, I realized that the natural progression for the child, with continued physical contact and stimulation from mother, was toward independence, not dependence. Probably this was because the baby was given security and every affirmation of belonging that the mother was able to give. In the infant's most vulnerable time, the mother carried and nursed the child, and during the rapid developments of the first year, the mother stimulated the child. With such security of self and place the child was able to feel inwardly confident enough to begin exploring outwardly on his own.

Perhaps because these children knew that their calls would be responded to, as they had been since infancy, they felt less inclined to call as a way of testing for a response from

mother & child

(OPPOSITE) Looking for fish in the spring-fed stream.

(THIS PAGE) Manda shows that he knows how to handle his camel.

adults. It had been firmly demonstrated that their needs would be met: they had not been left alone to cry, and they were carried and nurtured at all times. Therefore the child grew with the strong assumption that this support would continue.

A wonderful result of this self-confidence was the strong bond of friendship between peers. Self-assured children are less likely to be aggressive, need less supervision, and are more interested in playing together. I noticed intimate friendships lasting through the years in these small, close societies.

CHILDREN SECURE IN THEIR
WAYS IN MONGOLIA

FAR OUT ON THE MONGOLIAN PLAINS, I met Dawa. He and his parents lived with their extended family in gers, or yurts—portable homes that enable them to travel in search of fresh pastures for their goats, sheep, cows, and horses. Mongolian herders like Dawa's family were known for the beautiful horses that they raised and their ability to ride them. They live in rhythm with the seasons and in harmony with the land and the animals. The laws of nature govern their nomadic, pastoral lives, which in turn leaves these people with a deep respect and reverence for the natural world.

Early in the morning, just before sunrise, Dawa would wake up when his mother, Genma, rose to stoke their tiny stove with dried cow dung. She was always up first, warming the ger before bustling outside to milk the cows. I was sleeping on the floor of the ger and could see Dawa watching his mother go about her duties as he pulled his bed covers up to his cheeks. Genma didn't direct Dawa to rise and dress before she left the ger, nor did she assemble his clothes for dressing when she came back in with a pan

of warm, fresh milk. What I did notice was that Dawa and his mother quietly kept an eye on each other.

Dawa slid out of his bed and began pulling on trousers over his underclothes; then he huddled by the stove. The ger was losing the chill that had crept in during the night when the fire was not stoked. Dawa emptied the pot and sprinkled in tea to boil with the milk. His mother

looked on but didn't say a word; there was no need as long as Dawa was managing on his own. Myatav, Dawa's father, had slipped out to bring in his saddle so that he could inspect it for needed repairs while he sipped his morning tea.

Dawa's grandfather and his uncle, aunt, and cousin Olana were also having their morning tea in the other ger. They all traveled together, herding their animals on horseback and moving to a new site every few weeks. But life on the plains also had a daily routine: milking morning and evening, with repairs, food preparation, and collecting fuel for the stove going on during the day. Occasionally, as he would do today, Myatav would leave and round up the horses to bring them to auction.

I surmised that the casual observation Genma made of her son, Dawa, was something she had done ever since he had begun to stray

mother & child

from her on his own. Not wanting to meddle too much and interfere with Dawa's own problem solving, she had allowed Dawa to gain self-esteem through the sweat and frustration of figuring things out for himself. However, Genma was always there to lend a hand when Dawa needed and asked for it. She still kept her eye on him, ready to assist, which she did when Dawa called out as the handle on the pot of tea came off. Dawa was not hesitant to call, nor was Genma slow in responding. Although Dawa was very competent for a young child, he was still a child, and Genma responded appropriately, not with scolding but with assistance and direction.

Out on the grasslands where Dawa lived, there were no roads as far as the eye could see. In a beautiful, wild, natural setting such as this, a child like Dawa naturally

develops independence and self-reliance because he must have these qualities to live out on the land as an adult. I could see that a certain strength of character was needed for this rugged life on the grasslands. One needed to carry on regardless of weather, and there were no vacations or great luxuries.

I saw this strength of character developing early in life with Dawa, who acknowledged with his fingers that he was five years old. Although Dawa exhibited his love for his parents often by exchanging affectionate sniffs—the Mongolian equivalent of kissing—he was very content to go about his tasks undirected and on his own. Still childlike in his attitude and play, Dawa had a solid demeanor when executing a task; he was undaunted although still very much a child. Elements outside of Dawa's control, like the chilly temperature, or the early hour of the day, or the distance and time involved in the task, seemed to be taken in stride almost without notice.

Myatav and some of the other men were preparing to herd some of their horses into Ulan Bator, the capital of Mongolia, to sell or trade. I watched Myatav take the small saddle from Dawa and strap it onto a shorter, huskier horse tied in front of the family gers. It was evident that this horse was for Dawa. I watched in amazement while Dawa launched himself into his saddle. He grabbed the reins and the saddle above his head, stuck one foot on the side of the horse's leg, pulled himself up onto the back of the horse so that he could put his foot in the stirrup, and swung himself around into the saddle.

Dawa untied his horse, and after waving to Genma, who was standing outside the ger watching, he rode toward the men on horseback. His poise and self-confidence were inspiring. Genma had not been standing next to him relaying directions or even cautioning him about his efforts. At first this surprised me. I

then saw that the act of placing the saddle on the horse was the protective aspect of the scenario. The child was limited by this act because he could not physically do it himself. But as soon as it had been decided that Dawa should ride and his horse was saddled, then Dawa was given the privilege and responsibility of being in charge of himself without being told "Be careful" or "Watch out."

Myatav rode his large, stately horse toward Dawa and directed him to round the outside of the herd of horses the men had brought in. This put Dawa in position to start driving the herd forward. It was encouraging to see Dawa respond to a simple, non-verbal cue. Here, out on the Mongolian plains, in the herdsman's society, it was merely expected that a child could perform responsibly when given the chance. In no way did I ever see Dawa pushed to achieve, or not allowed to play like every other child in the world, but when Dawa wished to participate he was always given the opportunity, and was respected for it.

The children here seemed to live up to positive expectations. I wondered whether it could also be true that a parent who continually warned a child of danger and disaster could bring about that result. The Mongolian mothers whom I met couldn't be accused of being overprotective of their children. Yet they were always responsive and attentive, patiently waiting when their child's first efforts took a long time, yet not interfering unless asked. This permitted the child to feel in control of a new situation; the mother participated only as much as the child wished. I noticed that Genma watched as Dawa climbed into the saddle—but from the doorway of the ger. And she waved to him as he rode off, signaling not so much a warm good-bye as that she was there and would always be there in time of need.

Dawa's self-confidence helps him to develop the strong bond of friendship.

The men left with the horses for Ulan Bator after Dawa had herded the horses with them near the gers. Although Dawa was not going to ride for days onward with the men, he still was eager to ride on his own for a bit longer. Dawa neck-reined his horse around toward the river with confidence. He would take his horse down for a drink before bringing him in for the day. He was like many of the indigenous children I had met, who needed little

reassurance because they had grown up with close physical contact and attention from their mothers in their earliest, most vulnerable stages. Because of his secure background, at five years of age Dawa was already becoming quite independent.

6

individuality

A natural product of independence is individuality. As a child
ventures out on her own, she makes independent choices, which
chart her individual path. This in turn enables her unique personality to emerge. As a child grows, it becomes apparent which
tasks come more naturally, which ones are performed with greater
ease. A task well done does much to create high self-esteem. An
independent child with strong self-esteem, a child who knows
her own abilities, is beautiful.

   The preadolescent indigenous children that I spent time with
had much to teach me. It was through their patience and guidance that I was able to manage in these foreign environments. I

The Yanomama fish in hot mud ponds with bows and arrows. Bubbles and slight movements indicate where the fish are.

came to understand how they had been taught by their mothers because the same lessons were passed on to me as I learned how to interact and to survive in their natural world. I spent days with them in silent communication, participating in their daily routines and inadvertently learning about their unique personalities. They had reached a point in their lives where they brought their mothers' attentive lessons back to the community. The responsibilities they shouldered said much about their personalities and their individual talents. These directed and focused children were fun and enlightening to be with.

mother & child

Kari shows her younger sister how to drop the hay for the reindeer to eat.

SELF-ESTEEM OF THE OLDER CHILDREN WITH THE
SAMIS OF THE ARCTIC AND THE YANOMAMA OF THE AMAZON

THE SAMIS living above the Arctic circle must contend with the cold weather and all the extra efforts that come with it. Because of the reindeer native to this area, the Samis have plenty of meat to eat as well as skin and fur for clothing. In the springtime the Samis are busy herding their reindeer over the last of the snow toward the summer pastures for good grazing.

I met Karen and her daughter Kari during the annual spring celebration, which coincides with the movement of the reindeer. Karen told me that this festival of reindeer races and games of skill precedes the beautiful summer of the midnight sun. Her fondest memory as a child was the magical feeling of traveling on  a sled all night long under the low-lying sun as her family herded reindeer across the plateau. Karen herself was born in a lavu, which is very much like a Native

American tepee. Her traditional Sami upbringing was in tune with nature and the animals they lived with on the plateau.

Because Karen had been raised out on the land, she was able to teach her daughter Kari the traditional Sami ways of life, even though the modern world surrounded them. Kari was a sharp, quiet girl, and I noticed that she had been intently watching the older boys racing sleds drawn by their fastest reindeer. She

mother & child

had approached the time when she could begin driving the deer herself, and she was acquiring skills by keen observation.

Kari was not one to let on just how much she knew, but she went about her chores of her own accord, with confidence and often alone. It wasn't leadership she sought, but quiet competence. It was evident that she had learned by direct participation and a sort of osmosis from her mother. Kari was eager to show me her herd dog and sled, and as I had experienced before, she took charge of teaching me as she had been taught—by example.

Although springtime was joyous because of the return of the sun and the longer days and warmer temperatures, it was also a busy time because as the snows tended to become soft and slushy by day, they froze into a hard, clear surface by night. This could be a problem because the easy traveling at night for the reindeer caused them to spread out and wander in many directions. For this reason Kari's family was anxious to herd the reindeer quickly to the summer pastures before they dispersed. Kari knew this and was eager to do as her mother had when she was a girl: to be up at any time to travel with the reindeer.

INDIVIDUALITY

We had been out for a few hours circling the herd to gather the reindeer together. The air was cooling and the snow was beginning to harden. Color spread across the sky as the sun dipped lower. Kari came by me with the sled, holding the reins in her hands, and beckoned for me to ride with her. This was the first time I had seen her take charge, and it appeared to come naturally to her. Her father, out

on foot, was separating out a couple of deer that belonged to another family. They had a slightly different marking on the ear that indicated ownership.

Without any fanfare Kari was showing me what she could do. She carried her individuality with a subtle grace. I wrapped my legs around her as I sat behind her on the sled. When we took off, I had to laugh as the reindeer kicked bits of snow up into our faces. This did not deter Kari; she held the reins fast and directed our course.

Her father hopped on the runners on the back of the sled and held on. The sky was bright and streaked with color, our spirits were high, and Kari's father began to joik. Joiking is a form of song much like a yodel, but everyone has a personal joik—a song of the spirit. I sensed that Kari felt happy and quite proud to be driving the sled. She, like her mother, loved being out in the snow in the sled, driving the reindeer. Kari's accomplishments were becoming the same as those of

mother & child

her mother. Simply working by her mother's side had taught Kari how to handle and navigate the reindeer. She had been around these animals all through her childhood, and now her mother's teachings were bearing fruit: Kari's confidence and competence in driving and herding the reindeer were her gifts to the community.

INDIVIDUALITY

IN QUITE A DIFFERENT ENVIRONMENT from the Arctic Circle, the heart of the triple canopy rain forest of the Amazon territory teems with life. Orchid plants elegantly wrap themselves around trees; huge, colorful butterflies flit through the tangle of greenery; many rivers and streams weave through hundreds of miles of virgin jungle. Here nature is still allowed to care for herself. Without any synthetic influences from the outside, she recycles and rejuvenates herself beautifully. This is where the Yanomama live, the largest primitive tribe still remaining on earth.

A Yanomama's life is somewhat relaxed, considering that only about two hours every day are needed for fishing, foraging, or tending gardens. Life moves slowly

mother & child

for the people of this tribe, who have no words for time of day other than high noon, haven't invented the wheel, and still hunt with a bow and arrow. They live in extended family groups numbering fifty to one hundred in large, round, open-roofed, thatched homes called shaponos.

Occasionally they travel in groups through the jungle on wayumi, or hunt, often in search of meat such as tapir, armadillo, or deer.

When I visited a shapono on my own, the first to befriend me was a boy named Yapaperwe. The young ones became my guides and teachers when I lived with an indigenous group, perhaps because they had the time, patience, and fresh curiosity. I hung my hammock alone, near Yapaperwe's family's hammocks and fire, which delineated their individual living space as part of the whole shapono. Yapaperwe came to me and beckoned for me to come with him.

I was grateful for the invitation and wordlessly followed him through the communal garden of pineapple, sugar cane, papaya, bananas, plantains, yucca, and more. He showed me where they found the berries and roots that they ate as well. By this time we had a herd of smaller children following along. It was evident that they all respected and admired Yapaperwe, because they were quick to mind his

requests. Yapaperwe shouldered the responsibility of being their leader, which is probably why he had been the one to approach me in the first place.

Yapaperwe had become an individual of note for the other children. His personality and abilities were strong and apparent. The younger ones badgered him to demonstrate his skill with the bow and arrow so that they could observe

mother & child

and learn, and of course so that he could show off to me the hunting skills their tribe is known for. I was more interested in watching the intrigued, intent faces of the children studying Yapaperwe's movements than in watching the demonstration itself.

I could see that as Yapaperwe made his way toward adulthood, situations like this one reinforced his place in the tribe and shaped his individual personality. We pushed our way through the thick greenery down to a cool, spring-fed stream to escape the heat of the day. Yapaperwe grabbed one of the many vines dangling from a tree and swooped across the water. We all followed suit, slapping the water with our  feet and often falling in. Although Yapaperwe was keenly responsible, his sense of childlike fun was still quite intact.

We ran through the usual warm afternoon rain to the shapono, and a long, curving rainbow appeared across the sky. Shortly after we arrived the rain ceased, and everyone began singing and dancing heris, or songs of daily life and gratitude, together. Song is an integral part of a Yanomama's life. With arms linked, people danced long into the night. I drifted off to sleep and woke off and on to hear the shaman chanting in the wee hours.

At daybreak I had the most beautiful awakening I have ever had. In the mist, glowing a faint yellow, the shapes of the jungle began to take form around me. A slow melodic song floated in and out of my waking dreams. This music had a warm familiarity for me. As I became more aware that the day had begun and that I was part of it, I recognized the voice singing this gentle wake-up call to all the people of the shapono. It was Yapaperwe. He was circling the shapono as the sun met the dark sky, singing to bring us all into the day together.

He had been a little too shy to sing solo for me when the other children had sung, even though they had encouraged him to. I was surprised at his reticence, which seemed uncharacteristic to me, because he had exhibited such unshakable confidence all day. But this bit of shyness was endearing. This morning song, which I listened to with pleasure each and every morning during my visit, was Yapaperwe's way of overcoming his shyness and demonstrating his qualities of leadership at the same time. This task allowed Yapaperwe to express his individuality and gave him a place of distinction in the extended family group living in the shapono. The song was part of Yapaperwe's definition of himself.

7

mother as grandmother

There comes a time when a mother's children have children of
their own. A mother becomes a grandmother, and her role
changes. She becomes the keeper and carrier of the knowledge
that was passed on to her by her mother—the knowledge she
has garnered through her years of experience. Mothering is a
continuum; mothering is a process, an art.

I have such respect for the indigenous grandmothers I have
met. Their strength of character and generosity of spirit sustain
many family members. They have a quiet way of transferring
great amounts of knowledge, teaching their grandchildren di-
rectly by spending time with them, spinning yarns, and caring

for them. These women are the link between what was and what is now. If mother is the heart of the continuum, grandmother is the soul.

Grandmother preserves and maintains her culture for all her people by bridging the gap between past and present in mind, body, and spirit. Infusing daily life for her family and friends with the timeless essence of tradition, Grandmother is the source of cultural stability.

Whether in a bark shelter by the mangrove swamp, a reindeer skin tent, a stone yersa hut, or an igloo, Grandmother has learned how to create a simple home with available material out in the natural environment. Because of this she has learned how to live in harmony with the natural world, in sync with the seasons, close to the

land and the animals. Along with the stories and the rites of her culture, Grandmother passes on the lessons of Mother Nature, the greatest grandmother and teacher of all.

GRANDMOTHER AS THE LINK TO THE CONTINUUM WITH
THE SHERPAS IN THE HIMALAYA, THE ABORIGINES IN AUSTRALIA,
AND THE SAMIS AND INUIT OF THE ARCTIC

GRANDMOTHER, for many of the indigenous people, is as much a general term of affection and respect for all elder women as it is a specific term for their own kin. I admired the way my friends honored their elders by appreciating their gift of wisdom. With the Aborigines in Australia it was Grandmother who described the older cultural ways for me, just as she did for her own grandchildren.

Grandmother told me how to look, in order to truly see, when I was in the mangrove forest. Edible worms and mussels and more are to be found here, but so are snakes and crocodiles. This sixty-year-old woman walked deftly through the tangled mass, culling food for everyone, and was always very calm about the dangers. This never appeared to be a chore for her but always seemed to be a joy. The forest was where she wanted to be.

Amprenula, my Aboriginal friend, had a particular admiration for her grandmother, and it showed as they walked together through the bush. She seemed to listen a little more intently and accept advice a little more readily from her grandmother than from anyone else. It was as if she felt that if anyone would know, her grandmother would, because she had done this before many times.

Grandmother picked up a plant with something that looked like a long, condensed bud on the end. Since matches had entered their world this plant wasn't as important to the Aborigines as it had been in the past. Amprenula moved closer to take a look at the plant. The tip was glowing slightly red. Grandmother called it the fire stick, and with a wave of her hand and a touch of the plant wand, she set the dried grasses on fire.

When Grandmother was young, this plant was always carried and kept glowing, day and night. When one stick was about to burn out, another was lit from it. This was how people started their cooking fires and burned the thicker forests to clear the way for new green shoots to grow and attract animals to the area. Fire sticks were used every day, many times a day. Now Amprenula most often uses the conveniences of matches, but if need be she knows how to use a fire stick because of Grandmother.

High in the Himalaya the Sherpas are still surrounded by ancient traditions, and again I found Grandmother to be the family keeper of the traditional ways. Far up in the mountainous summer pastures, in the settlements of yersas— the small stone family dwellings used while the people are herding up high—I spent some time with a family grazing their yaks.

Everyone, including the children, would begin to stir very early as

mother & child

light cracked the sky. The family slept together on the floor, and often it was the older boy who would sleep next to his Grandmother. As the light made its way into the small hut, Grandmother would begin with her stories and her chants. The day began to take shape around the sleepy young boy, and I could see that Grandmother's strong and soothing presence had definite effects on him. It was almost as if Grandmother was gently leading him into the day, centering his life with tales and information that had shaped their culture for generation upon generation.

Each morning Grandmother gave the boy a sense of security and belonging as well as an identity—a definition of who he was in the larger world. Before long, after a hot cup of tea and some tsampa (ground barley), the boy ran out to bring the yaks to the hut for their morning milking. His active day had begun. Grandmother's influence was simple and almost unconscious, like a waking dream. The boy's life was his own as he moved about in his independent play and chores; yet his heritage was intact because of his grandmother.

Back in the trade village of Namche Bazar I came to know my friend Mingma's grandmother. She and her husband still spent their days weaving rugs in old Tibetan patterns. The great-grandchildren ran freely in and out of their simple home, drinking cups of tea and warming themselves at the hearth. All the while, Grandmother would be twirling her prayer wheel, chanting, filling her sacred bowls with water for the spirits. Grandmother carried her deep sense of ritual throughout the day. Although she did not impose it on the children, it was in the background of their everyday lives. Grandmother's sense of the sacred exposed the children to respect for the spirit of life in all people and in the land and the waters.

They learned from Grandmother that the spirit of life in all things connected them to all that exists in the natural world. But these concepts were taught so quietly and indirectly that the grandchildren and great-grandchildren learned without conscious effort, and so did I.

Above the Arctic Circle I herded reindeer with the Samis. I had spent time herding our cows on the dairy farm where I grew up, but this was a little different. These animals were neither wild nor tame. They accepted our presence but were lively and skittish when we worked together to move them in a particular direction. I needed to watch and listen to direction to be really helpful, but Grandmother was there to show me what to do.

Although she was hardly as quick as anyone else, Grandmother demonstrated that she could still be effective. But more importantly, she showed me and all the others, including the children, that participation in the roundup was what really mattered. Grandmother broke off a small tree branch and stationed herself at a strategic point, knowing from past experience where the reindeer

were likely to run. Then, at the critical moment, she began waving and thwacking with her branch.

Grandmother was there in person but had an even larger presence in spirit. The children could see what a sport she was, how her knowledge over the years enabled her to be effective, and how her participation

lifted the spirits of all the others herding alongside her. Taking part was the most valuable thing a person could do, regardless of ability. That was Grandmother's most important message.

It is easy enough to describe what has value for Grandmother in her twilight years. She is seldom trapped by ego and vanity. When I saw Grandmother affectionately peering into her lovely granddaughter's eyes, her action told me a story of fleeting beauty and youth. Youth is nothing worth clinging to; it is not who you are; it does not sing with your spirit as your actions do. Participating wholeheartedly in life and family, in culture and tradition, has allowed Grandmother to become the individual she is and an example for her grandchildren to love.

The Inuit grandmother I met showed me something: a type of singing that sounds like the breath of angels. It is an unearthly sound, unlike anything I had heard before. Perhaps part of the reason it was so unusual was the acoustics of the igloo—the snow dome that surrounded us.

mother & child

Only Grandmother and her peers were able to create this audible sensation in a game called kayavak, which they had played together as children and had perfected as they grew older. I was sitting with the children in the igloo. We were warm and toasty in our caribou skins as we listened intently. None of the children knew how to kayavak, probably because they were exposed to it so seldom these days, but now they sat with rapt attention.

MOTHER AS GRANDMOTHER

Grandmother took a big old pot and raised it to her face and her friend's face. She took a deep breath and began sounding into the pot. As rapidly as she could, she articulated breathy syllables without pausing for intake of air. She incorporated her breathing into the rhythmic sound she was making. Her friend was repeating each syllable after her just as rapidly, like a high-speed, airy round. The competition and the fun was for Grandmother to go so fast that she would trip up her friend's tongue, or herself.

These two women would go on for several minutes before one or the other broke into laughter. When Grandmother was young this song game had entertained extended family groups and strengthened friendships on many a cold night. Through Grandmother and her game the children were learning that amidst tremendous cold weather and the hardships of daily life, one can create the spirit of fun and friendship, easing the burdens of life.

As I listened to this beautiful, unearthly music, I realized how all in the igloo looked to Grandmother for her spirited and insightful guidance. Her knowledge gives direction and stability to their lives and ensures the continuation of the tribe, but she offers more than that. She represents the continuity between generations: the link between mother and mother, between mother and child.

mother & child

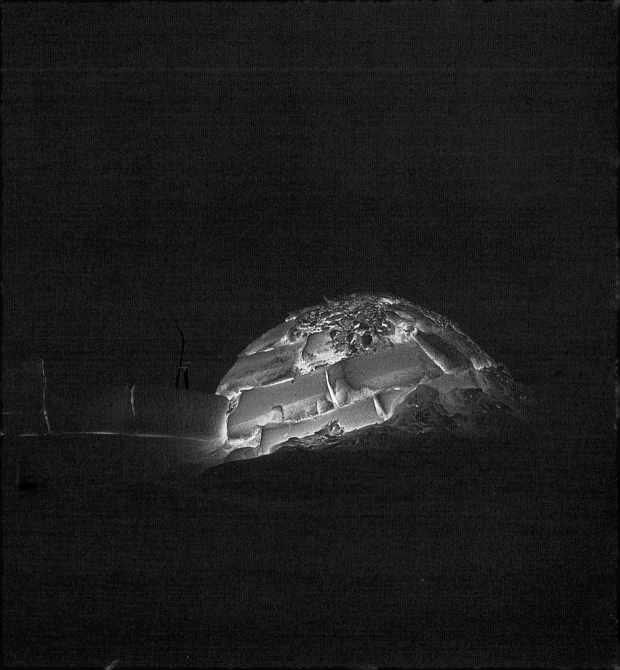

afterword

OUR MODERN LIVES have complexities that often leave us searching for simple lifestyle solutions. These accounts of indigenous women and how they handle their children in a natural setting may seem romantic, or entertaining at best. How do they apply to us in our fast-paced, materially oriented world?

I wasn't aware of how applicable the ways of my indigenous friends were until I had a child of my own. Although our societies were different, I found that when I had a lifestyle decision to make, thinking of these indigenous women and their natural methods enabled me to arrive at workable, caring solutions. These women unknowingly convinced me that the best guide for handling my own child was not a particular schedule or book but my own natural instincts. They gave me the confidence to trust in myself because they trusted themselves, and I had seen the wonderful impact this had on their children.

I needed to adapt indigenous methods to make them work in my life, but keeping their ways in mind helped me to create fresh options that might not have been initially obvious or readily available. For example, when I was pregnant, I remembered my friends who lived simple lives in situations that we, in our society, might view as very hard. It was merely part of normal, everyday life to haul water in the Himalaya, travel on camel caravan in the Sahara, and gather food in the jungle in the Amazon basin. Bearing this in mind, I headed off to Morocco to climb and ski Mount Toubkal for a couple of work projects of my own. I checked with several doctors who had high-altitude experience, as well as my local doctor, and all concluded that the elevation was no problem as long as I didn't push myself aerobically. Because this sort of activity was common for me before I was carrying my child, it was acceptable while I was pregnant. I had even climbed this peak before and knew the route well. My indigenous friends had always continued their chores when pregnant, while living in yurts, stone huts, or tent-like structures. Why shouldn't I continue my tasks as long as there was no danger to my child? I climbed slowly, never getting out of breath, and snowboarded down with an ice ax ready to prevent any slips.

I learned from Mingma, Genma, and others to maintain my lifestyle while pregnant. I encourage other women to confer with their physicians; chances are they will not have to stop any activity altogether. The idea is not to overdo anything—to moderate activities to accommodate the body's changing shape.

My husband and I decided to have our child at home with a midwife, and we were fortunate to have excellent backup medical facilities at a nearby hospital in case complications arose. I found that I could experience all the intimacies that Mingma had while giving birth at home, but my society gave me protective choices not available for Mingma, and I was thankful for this.

Because I had observed nursing around the world, I knew that it is a natural bonding instinct and that I would nurse my child. However, the reality isn't always so simple. I had recurring problems with breast infections but was convinced that both the medical and emotional benefits for my child would make it more than worthwhile to work out problems with mastitis. If a woman finds nursing difficult, family members may have pertinent advice, or a state health agency can connect her with the many different women's groups that support breastfeeding.

Working mothers can express milk with the many varieties of pumps available, choosing the option of breastfeeding while working away from home. The baby's caretaker merely feeds yesterday's expressed milk so that mother and baby can stay in their delicate feeding balance. Before a mother decides that nursing is just plain inconvenient, she should make a quick call to a nursing support group—they can help her work out the details of her schedule.

Because I had seen women around the world carrying their babies close to their bodies at all times, I looked into carrying accoutrements right away. What proved to be the most immediately useful was a sling with a comfortable shoulder pad and a plastic D-ring for adjusting the amount of pouch needed to rest the baby in comfort. While using the sling I had relative freedom during my days, whether preparing food in the kitchen or walking to the stream for a dip. The sling also allowed me to nurse unobtrusively by pulling the fabric over the baby at the breast.

When my child was two months old I had to lecture in Prague, and I forgot to pack my sling. I thought about what my indigenous friends had used, and improvisation became easy. Walking outside in the streets, I slid him inside my jacket, facing out to watch the world. Inside, I used material tied like a sling for an injured arm to carry him next to me. This way my arms were free for my own needs.

Because many women do not have the flexibility that I have with my work, they may feel they cannot stay close to their infants during the early months. Creativity comes into play now: perhaps working less and doing with less money is a viable option. Again, the influence of the indigenous caused me to let go of the notion of purchasing a crib and many other baby specialty items. I knew that my women friends who lived simple lives merely incorporated their children into their existing lifestyles—things didn't change drastically with the new baby.

Without these extra purchases I brought our newborn into our own bed, saved money, and gained sleep by simply rolling over to nurse in the night. For generations, families around the world have slept this way, and I found that it worked well for us too, especially when traveling for work.

But for those who absolutely have to return to work, looking at both parents' schedules might give rise to some flexibility. If a mother can work side by side with her child, all the better. If asked, an employer might allow a mother to bring her child to work, or work at home part of the week when her child is still young.

Mothers coordinating with other moms—swapping childcare for free time— is one option. I arranged to share an older teenager who was working as a live-in with a friend. Our children would spend time at each of our homes but with the same teenage caretaker. This worked well because the children had playmates for fun, learned to get along, and still had the consistency of the same caretaker. And each of us had a chance to have the children in our own homes.

Commercial day care can be quite good if this is a chosen option. It is important to check the ratio of children to caregivers (opting for the lowest) and to visit for observation, perhaps starting with shorter amounts of time and allowing the child to know her caretaker before leaving her for full days.

Soon, perhaps all too soon, children will be so grown up that they will show great signs of secure independence. I felt happy and relieved to see my son say "Bye" with a big smile when I left him with our shared caretaker. But there is always the wistful feeling of wanting to be needed more. My indigenous friends taught me that their job as mothers was to teach their children, from the moment of birth, to live without them.

I learned the lesson of letting go while watching indigenous children. For the most part, the chfldren solved their own curiosities and settled their own griev-ances in a group. There is great temptation to jump in and untangle a problem for a child, but unless they invite a parent in to give them some direction, it is often best to let them work it out. This way they experience their own successes and learn that they can achieve on their own. Through these small successes the child's personality develops, bringing to light the skills that come naturally. Eventually, responsibilities that correlate with these skills and talents will gravitate to the child, and their performance will add to the child's self-esteem. The foundation for a child's life is built during its earliest, most vulnerable stages. I looked for role models to support my decisions when caring for my own child. Because I had seen how happy and effective the older indigenous children were within their commu-nity, I came to trust and appreciate the simple, instinctual ways of their mothers. Keeping these women in mind has been a great heartfelt reassurance to me. Adapting my lifestyle to incorporate some of their ways has made my life with my child more meaningful.